The Ultimate Waffles Cookbook

Delicious Waffle Recipes

The Best Waffle Iron Recipes You Will Ever Get Across

BY

Rachael Rayner

Copyright 2016 Rachael Rayner

License Notes

No part of this Book can be reproduced in any form or by any means including print, electronic, scanning or photocopying unless prior permission is granted by the author.

All ideas, suggestions and guidelines mentioned here are written for informative purposes. While the author has taken every possible step to ensure accuracy, all readers are advised to follow information at their own risk. The author cannot be held responsible for personal and/or commercial damages in case of misinterpreting and misunderstanding any part of this Book

About The Author

Rachael Rayner

Are you tired of cooking the same types of dishes over and over again? As a mother of not one, but two sets of twins, preparing meals became very challenging, very early on. Not only was it difficult to get enough time in the kitchen to prepare anything other than fried eggs, but I was constantly trying to please 4 little hungry mouths under 5 years old. Of course I would not trade my angels for anything in the world, but I had just about given up on cooking, when I had a genius idea one afternoon while I was napping beside one of my sons. I am so happy and proud to tell you that since then, my kitchen has become my sanctuary and my children have become my helpers. I have transformed my meal preparation, my grocery shopping habits, and my cooking style. I am Racheal Rayner, and I am proud to tell you that I am no longer the boring mom sous-chef people avoid. I am the house in our neighborhood where every kid (and parent) wants to come for dinner.

I was raised Jewish in a very traditional household, and I was not allowed in the kitchen that much. My mother cooked the same recipes day in day out, and salt and pepper were probably the extent of the seasonings we were able to detect in the dishes she made. We did not even know any better until we moved out of the house. My husband, Frank is a foodie. I thought I was too, until I met him. I mean I love food, but who doesn't right? He revolutionized my knowledge about cooking. He used to take over in the kitchen, because after all, we were a modern couple and both of us worked full time jobs. He prepared chilies, soups, chicken casseroles—one more delicious than the last. When I got pregnant with my first set of twins and had to stay home on bed rest, I took over the kitchen and it was a disaster. I tried so hard to find the right ingredients and recipes to make the dishes taste something close to my husband's. However, I hated follow recipes. You don't tell a pregnant woman that her food tastes bad, so Frank and I reluctantly ate the dishes I prepared on week days. Fortunately, he was the weekend chef.

After the birth of my first set of twins, I was too busy to even attempt to cook. Sure, I prepared thousands of bottles of milk and purees, but Frank and I ended up eating take out 4 days out of 5. Then, no break for this mom, I gave birth to my second set of twins only 19 months later! I knew that now it was not just about Frank and I anymore, but it was about these little ones for whom I wanted to cook healthy meals, and I had to learn how to cook.

One afternoon in March, when I got up from that power nap with my boys, I had figured out what I needed to do to improve my cooking skills and stop torturing my family with my bland dishes. I had to let go of everything I had learned, tasted, or seen from my childhood and start over. I spent a week organizing my kitchen, and I equipped myself a new blender. I also got some fun shaped cookie cutters, a rolling pin, wooden spatulas, mixing bowls, fruit cutters, and plenty of plastic storage containers. I was ready.

My oldest twins, Isabella and Sophia are now teenagers, and love to cook with their Mom when they are not too busy talking on the phone. My youngest twins Erick and John, are now 10 years old and so helpful in the kitchen, especially when it's time to make cookies.

Let me start sharing my tips, recipes, and shopping suggestions with you ladies and gentlemen. I did not reinvent the wheel here but I did make my kitchen my own, started storing my favorite baking ingredients, and visiting the fresh produce market more often. I have mastered the principles of slow cooking and chopping veggies ahead of time. I have even embraced the involvement of my little ones in the kitchen with me.

I never want to hear you say that you are too busy to cook some delicious and healthy dishes, because BUSY, is my middle name.

Table of Contents

Introduction

Who doesn't love the taste of delicious waffles in the morning? Waffles in general are one of the most versatile breakfast dishes that you can make. You can easily make different types of waffles such as delicious blueberry waffles, healthy banana waffles, sweet tasting chocolate chip waffles or even chicken and waffles sandwiches. There is no end to any type of waffle that you can make and you can always make a waffle dish that fits your taste buds or that will help satisfy those picky eaters in your household.

If you are a huge fan of waffles and have been looking for a waffle cookbook to help you make some of the most delicious waffle recipes possible, then you have certainly come to the right book. Inside of this book you will discover not only a few useful tips to making some of the most delicious waffles you will ever taste, but you will also discover over 25 over the most delicious and unique waffle recipes you will ever find.

So, whether you are a fan of traditional Belgian waffles or have been looking for a more creative and different waffle recipe such as a chicken and waffle sandwich, you can rest assured you will find it inside of this book.

So, let's not waste any more time!

Let's get cooking!

Making The Perfect Waffles Each and Every Time

There is no one way to make a delicious waffle. There are a variety of different ways that you can make waffles and every way that you make them is unique in its own right. In this section I want to give you a few helpful tips to making perfect waffles each and every time.

1. Make Sure That You Respect Your Waffle Maker

If there is one thing that you need to make sure that you do first and all of the time is to respect your specific waffle maker. All waffle makers are designed to cook your waffles differently and as such you want to make sure that you read your manual for the unit the moment that you purchase it. Each manual will give you different advice on how to make delicious waffles so make sure that you read the manual in its entirety.

2. The True Meaning of Non-Stick

When it comes to making waffles one of the things that many people tend to get confused is whether or not they should add cooking spray to the waffle maker. Well, this can be determined by reading the manual I suggested in the first step. It can also help you to be aware of how much oil or butter that you use in your batter. This will allow you to have in mind if your waffle will stick your waffle maker as it is cooking.

With that in mind if you are always making waffles that tend to stick to your waffle maker no matter what you do differently, I highly recommend that you increase the oil or butter that you use.

3. Always Separate the Yolks from The Whites

If you are striving to have a light and fluffy waffle, then the perfect thing for you to do is to separate your eggs. Always add in your egg yolks to your batter first and then beat your egg whites in a separate bowl until peaks begin to form on the surface. Once these peaks form, gently fold in your egg whites into your final batter.

4. Avoid Over Mixing

Waffle batter itself is very tricky and it always should be smooth in consistency. However, you want to make sure that you never make waffle batter that is over mixed. The only real solution to preventing this from happening is to have great patience. Instead of using an electric mixer I highly recommend that you use a rubber spatula and when you stir your mixture together to form your final batter only make sure to do so until your batter is moist and smooth in consistency.

5. Not Using Buttermilk?

There are many recipes out there for waffle and many of these recipe will call for buttermilk and many people just don't use it oftentimes. The problem with using buttermilk is that a lot of people don't keep it around or have it handy whenever they are making waffles. This can be easily remedied by simply replacing it with regular milk. The main difference that you will notice is that texture is slightly different but it is not drastically so.

However, if you are dying for the taste of tangy buttermilk in your waffles I highly recommend adding at least a tablespoon of vinegar or fresh lemon juice to your cup of milk. This acidity will cause the milk to curdle slightly and if you leave it for at least 15 minutes before adding it into your batter it will give your waffles the same taste as if you had use buttermilk in the first place.

6. Never Lift the Lid of Your Waffle Maker too Early

As a general rule you always want to make sure that you wait until the indicator light is flashing or beeping mechanism is beeping before you lift the lid of your waffle maker to check on your waffles. Lifting the lid too early on your waffle maker can cause your waffle to rip cleanly in half or leaving it stuck to one side of the maker.

7. Preventing Over Cooking

If your waffle maker does not come with an indicator such as a beeping mechanism or a flashing light, all you have to do is watch the steam that is coming out of your unit as your waffles cook. Once this steam begins to stop, lift the lid of your waffle maker as your waffle should be done.

8. Always Eat at The Same Time as The Rest of Your Family

If you are making waffles for many people and are afraid that your waffles are going to get cold when everybody else is ready to eat, there is a simple solution for you. To keep all of your waffles warm at the same temperature so that they are ready for everybody in your home when everybody is ready to eat, just preheat your oven to 250 degrees at the same time that you preheat your oven maker. Once you are done cooking your waffles one-by-one, add them into your oven to keep them warm and this will actually help to improve the crunchiness of your waffles as well.

9. Never Waste Your Waffles

This is something you have probably been told since an early age and it is still true to this day. However, if you find that you have made yourself way too many waffles, all that you have to do is place them into your freezer the moment they are cold. Whenever you are ready to eat your leftovers set them out to defrost for about 10 minutes and then heat them right back up in your oven at a toasty 300 degrees for 5 minutes and they will taste just as if you had made them for fresh.

10. Clean Up

One of the best things that you can do to ensure quick and regrettable cleanup is to clean your waffle maker shortly after it has cooled down. This will make it much easier to clean and you will be more thankful for it in the long run.

11. Using Butter? Keep it Warm

If you are the type of person that enjoys waffles with a dollop of fresh butter on the top, I highly recommend that you warm up your butter by leaving it out at room temperature so that it can be smooth perfectly onto your waffle without ripping it in the process.

Delicious and Simple Waffle Recipes

Vegan Style S'more Waffles

This waffle dish will certainly pique your interest because it is a great tasting breakfast dish to make if you are looking for a sweet tasting treat to enjoy. These waffles are easy to make and will help to satisfy any picky eater.

Makes: 4 Servings

Total Prep Time: 20 Minutes

Ingredients for Your Mushroom Fluff:

- ½ Cup of Chickpea, Brine
- ¾ tsp. of Guar Gum
- ½ tsp. of Lemon Juice, Fresh
- ½ Cup of Sugar, Powdered Variety
- 2 tsp. of Vanilla, Powdered

Ingredients for Your Waffles:

- 1 ¼ Cup of Flour, Buckwheat Variety
- 1 Cup of Flour, Oat Variety
- 2/3 Cup of Rice Flour, Sweet Variety
- 1 ½ Tbsp. of Baker's Style Baking Powder
- 2 tsp. of Cinnamon, Ground Variety
- ½ tsp. of Allspice
- ½ tsp. of Salt, For Taste
- 1 1/3 Cup + ¼ Cup of Milk, Non Dairy Variety
- 2 tsp. of Lemon Juice, Fresh
- 1/3 Cup of Applesauce

- 1/3 Cup of Oil, Sunflower Variety
- 1/3 Cup of Maple Syrup, Your Favorite Kind
- 1/3 Cup of Molasses, Blackstrap Variety
- 2 tsp. of Vanilla, Pure

Ingredients for Your Chocolate Sauce:

- 10 Dates, Medjool Variety and Pitted
- 1 Cup of Milk, Non Dairy Variety
- ¾ Cup of Chocolate Chips, Vegan Variety
- Dash of Salt, For Taste

Directions:

1. First combine your chickpea brine with your fresh lemon juice and guar gum in a large sized mixing bowl. Use an electric mixer and beat for the next 2 minutes or until thick in consistency.

2. Then add in your xylitol and powdered vanilla and mix again with your mixer until thick in consistency.

3. Next use a medium sized bowl and mix together your milk and lemon juice until evenly mixed. Set aside for later use. Add in your applesauce, oil, favorite type of syrup, pure vanilla and molasses and whisk thoroughly until combined.

4. Use a large sized separate bowl and mix together your buckwheat, rice, oats and almond flour until evenly mixed. Add in your baking powder, arrowroot, ground cinnamon, dash of salt and allspice. Stir again to mix

5. Mix your wet ingredients into your dry ingredients and use an electric mixer until a thick batter begins to form.

6. Preheat a waffle iron to high heat. Once it is hot enough scoop at least one cup of your batter onto it and allow to cook until completely done on both sides.

7. Top your cooked waffles with your marshmallow fluff and drizzle your chocolate sauce over the top. Serve immediately and enjoy.

Breakfast Style Waffle Tacos

With the help of this delicious recipe you never have to make a choice between a sweet and savory breakfast dish again. This dish is great for those looking to take a delicious dish along with them.

Makes: 4 Servings

Total Prep Time: 25 Minutes

Ingredients:

- 8 Waffles, Frozen Variety
- 8 Slices of Bacon, Thinly Sliced
- 8 Eggs, Large in Size and Whisked Thoroughly
- 1 Cup of Cheddar Cheese, while in Color and Finely Shredded
- Dash of Salt, For Taste
- Dash of Black Pepper, For Taste
- Some Maple Syrup, For Serving

Directions:

1. The first thing that you want to do is preheat your oven to 350 degrees. While your oven is heating up microwave your waffles for at least 25 seconds.

2. Then place your waffles between the slots of a turned over cupcake tin and place into your oven to bake for the next 5 minutes or until your waffles holds its shape.

3. Next use a large sized skillet placed over medium heat and cook up your bacon until it is crispy to the touch. Transfer to a plate lined with paper towels and allow to drain. Once cooled break your bacon in half.

4. Add your eggs to your skillet along with half of your bacon grease and cook until slightly scrambled.

5. Add in your cheese and stir thoroughly until melted. Remove from heat and season with a dash of salt and pepper.

6. Top your waffles with at least two bacon strips and your eggs.

7. Drizzle with some maple syrup and serve right away.

Cornbread Style Waffles

If you are looking for a southern style waffle recipe to make, then this is the perfect dish for you. The best part about this dish is that no baking is required on your part.

Makes: 6 Servings

Total Prep Time: 25 Minutes

Ingredients:

- 1 Cup of Buttermilk, Whole
- ½ Cup of Butter, Unsalted Variety and Fully Melted
- 6 Tbsp. of Sugar, White
- 2 Eggs, Large in Size and Beaten Lightly
- 1 Cup of Flour, All Purpose Variety
- 1 ½ Cup of Cornmeal, Yellow in Color
- 1 ½ tsp. of Baker's Style Baking Powder
- 1 tsp. of Baker's Style Baking Soda
- ¼ tsp. of Salt, For Taste
- 2 Tbsp. of Butter, Soft and for Serving
- 1 tsp. of Honey, Raw

Directions:

1. First preheat your waffle iron to high heat.

2. Next use a large sized bowl and whisk together your butter, sugar, whole buttermilk and eggs until evenly mixed.

3. Then add in your flour, cornmeal, dash of salt and baking soda. Stir thoroughly until evenly mixed together.

4. Spray your waffle iron with some cooking spray and scoop at least one fourth cup of your battery onto it. Cook for the next 5 minutes or until golden brown in color on both sides. Repeat until all of your batter has been used up.

5. Then mix together your honey and soft butter together until evenly mixed. Drizzle this over your warm waffles and enjoy.

Strawberry Cheesecake Style French Toast Waffles

If you are a huge fan of both French toast and waffles alike, then this is the perfect dish for you to make. It incorporates both of these tasty dishes to make one amazing breakfast dish you won't be able to deny.

Makes: 4 Servings

Total Prep Time: 35 Minutes

Ingredients:

- 8 Tbsp. of Cream Cheese, Soft
- 2 Tbsp. of Jam, Strawberry Variety
- ¼ Cup of Strawberries, Finely Chopped
- 2 Eggs, Large in Size and Beaten
- ½ Cup Milk, Whole
- ¼ tsp. of Nutmeg, Ground
- 1 Tbsp. of Sugar, White
- ½ tsp. of Cinnamon, Ground
- 8 Slices of Challah Bread
- Some Powdered Sugar, For Dusting
- Some Maple Syrup, For Serving and Your Favorite Kind

Directions:

1. The first thing that you want to do is make your cheesecake filling. To do this mix together your cream cheese, jam and chopped strawberries in a small sized bowl until evenly mixed.

2. Then use a separate medium sized bowl and whisk together your eggs, whole milk, sugar, ground cinnamon and nutmeg. Stir thoroughly to combine.

3. On one slice of your challah bread spread your cream cheese mixture over the top and top off with another slice. Repeat until all of your challah bread has been spread with cream cheese.

4. Place each of these sandwiches into your egg mixture and coat thoroughly.

5. Preheat your waffle iron to high heat and once it is hot enough spray with a generous amount of cooking spray.

6. Place your sandwich into your waffle iron and cook until golden brown in color.

7. Remove and top off with your favorite maple syrup and powdered sugar. Enjoy.

Pumpkin Spiced Waffles

If you have someone in your home that has a love for pumpkin, then this is the perfect recipe for you. With this recipe you can spoil this person the taste of pumpkin with a delicious breakfast treat they won't soon forget.

Makes: 7 to 8 Servings

Total Prep Time: 35 Minutes

Ingredients:

- 2 ½ Cups of Flour, All Purpose Variety
- 2 tsp. of Baker's Style Baking Powder
- ¾ tsp. of Baker's Style Baking Soda
- ¾ tsp. of Salt, For Taste
- 1 ½ tsp. of Cinnamon, Ground
- ½ tsp. of Ginger, Ground
- ¼ tsp. of Nutmeg, Ground
- 4 Eggs, Large in Size, Yolks and Whites Separated
- Dash of Cream of Tartar
- 5 Tbsp. of Sugar, Granulated Variety and Evenly Divided
- 1 Cup of Milk, Whole
- 1 Cup of Buttermilk, Whole
- ¼ Cup of Oil, Canola Variety
- 1 Cup of Pumpkin Puree, Canned Variety
- 1 tsp. of Vanilla, Pure
- Some Cooking Spray

- Some Maple Syrup, Apple Cider Variety and Butter Pecan Variety

Directions:

1. First preheat your oven to 225 degrees and preheat a waffle iron.

2. While both are heating up use a large sized mixing bowl and whisk together your flour, baking powder and soda, dash of salt, ground cinnamon, and nutmeg until thoroughly mixed together.

3. Make a small well in the center of your ingredients and set aside for later use.

4. Use a medium sized mixing bowl and whisk together your egg whites and cream of tartar. Use an electric mixer and continue to beat for the next 3 minutes or until soft peaks begin to form. Add in your sugar and continue to whisk until peaks begin to form again.

5. In a separate medium sized mixing bowl whisk together your milk, whole buttermilk, oil, pumpkin, vanilla, egg yolks and remaining sugar.

6. While you are whisking gently fold in your egg whites into your batter and pour this mixture into your flour mixture. Continue stirring until thoroughly combined.

7. Once your batter is ready pour at least one fourth cup of your batter onto your waffle iron and cook for at least 5 minutes or until golden brown in color.

8. Repeat until all of your batter has been used up and serve your waffles whenever you are ready.

Oreo Cheesecake Waffles

Here is yet another breakfast treat that the entire family will fall in love with. It is the perfect treat to serve up if someone in your house hold is a huge fan of Oreos. Feel free to serve this up for breakfast or for a special dessert treat.

Makes: 4 Servings

Total Prep Time: 30 Minutes

Ingredients for Your Waffles:

- 2 Cups of Flour, All Purpose Variety
- ½ Cup of Sugar, White
- 1 Tbsp. of Baker's Style Baking Powder
- 2 Tbsp. of Cocoa Powder
- 1 tsp. of Salt, For Taste
- 2 Eggs, Light and Packed
- 1 ½ Cups Milk, Whole
- 8 Tbsp. of Butter, Fully Melted
- 20 Oreo Cookies, Finely Crushed

Ingredients for Your Cheesecake Cream:

- 8 Ounces of Cream Cheese, Soft
- 1 Cup of Cream, Heavy Variety
- ½ Cup of Sugar, Powdered Variety
- 8 Oreo Cookies, Roughly Chopped
- Some Whipped Cream, For Topping

Directions:

1. First preheat your waffle iron to high heat.

2. Then use a large sized mixing bowl and mix together your flour, baking powder, dash of salt, white sugar and cocoa until evenly mixed together.

3. Add in your eggs and melted butter. Stir thoroughly until combined.

4. Gently fold in your crushed Oreos.

5. Once your batter is ready pour at least one fourth cup of your batter onto your waffle iron and cook for at least 5 minutes or until golden brown in color. Repeat until all of your batter has been used up.

6. Use a medium sized bowl and beat together your soft cream cheese until smooth in consistency.

7. Add in your powdered sugar as well as your heavy cream and continue to beat until soft peaks begin to form.

8. Spread at least one waffle with your cheesecake filling and then top off with another waffle. Repeat with your remaining waffles.

9. Top off with your chopped Oreos and whipped cream. Serve right away and enjoy.

Tasty Apple Fritter Wafflelets

If you love the taste of waffles and donuts, then this is one recipe you certainly need to try for yourself. This dish incorporates both the taste of donuts and waffles, to make a dish that you won't want to put down.

Makes: 16 Servings

Total Prep Time: 30 Minutes

Ingredients:

- 2 Cups of Flour, All Purpose Variety
- ¾ Cup of Sugar, Granulated Variety
- 2 tsp. of Baker's Style Baking Powder
- ½ tsp. of Baker's Style Baking Soda
- 1 tsp. of Salt, For Taste
- 2 tsp. of Cinnamon, Ground
- ¾ Cup of Buttermilk, Whole
- ¼ Cup of Butter, Unsalted Variety and Fully Melted
- 2 Eggs, Large in Size and Beaten
- 1 tsp. of Vanilla, Pure
- 2 Cups of Apples, Peeled and Finely Chopped
- Some Oil, Vegetable Variety

Ingredients for Your Glaze:

- 1 ½ Cup of Sugar, Powdered Variety
- ¼ Cup of Milk, Whole
- 2 tsp. of Vanilla, Pure

Directions:

1. Using a large sized bowl combine your flour, baking powder and soda, ground cinnamon, dash of salt and sugar until evenly mixed.

2. Gently add in your butter milk, eggs, soft butter and pure vanilla. Stir thoroughly to combine.

3. Gently fold in your chopped apples and stir until evenly incorporated.

4. Once your batter is ready pour at least one fourth cup of your batter onto your waffle iron and cook for at least 5 minutes or until golden brown in color. Repeat until all of your batter has been used up.

5. Next make your glaze. To do this mix together your powdered sugar, vanilla and milk in a small sized bowl until smooth in consistency and evenly mixed.

6. Dip your waffles into the glaze and set on a wire rack to chill for 20 minutes before serving.

Gluten Free Waffle Churros with Chocolate

Even if you do not celebrate Cinco de Mayo, this is one dish that you should enjoy anyway. The chocolate sauce served with this dish makes this dish even more delicious.

Makes: 4 to 8 Servings

Total Prep Time: 20 Minutes

Ingredients for Your Waffles:

- 1 ½ Cups of Milk, Whole
- 4 Tbsp. of Butter, Unsalted Variety and Finely Chopped
- 1/8 tsp. of Salt, For Taste
- 1 ¼ Cups of Flour, Gluten Free Variety
- ¼ Cup of Sugar, Granulated Variety
- 4 Eggs, Large in Size and at Room Temperature

Ingredients for Your Cinnamon and Sugar Coating:

- ½ Cup of Sugar, Granulated Variety
- 2 tsp. of Cinnamon, Ground
- 2 Tbsp. of Butter, Unsalted Variety and Melted

Ingredients for Your Chocolate Sauce:

- 4 Ounces of Chocolate, Bittersweet and Finely Chopped
- 1 ½ Cups of Milk, Whole
- 2 tsp. of Rice Flour, Fine and Sweet Variety

Directions:

1. The first thing that you want to do is make your waffle batter. To do this place your milk, butter and dash of salt into a medium sized saucepan and place over medium heat. Continue to cook until your butter is fully melted and it begins to boil.

2. Remove from heat and add in your flour, sugar and ground cinnamon. Stir thoroughly to combine.

3. Return to heat and continue to stir for the next 3 minutes. Remove from heat again and allow your mixture too cool for the next five minutes.

4. Transfer to a food processor and add in your eggs. Pulse thoroughly until your mixture is smooth in consistency.

5. Once your batter is ready pour at least one fourth cup of your batter onto your waffle iron and cook for at least 5 minutes or until golden brown in color. Repeat until all of your batter has been used up.

6. Next make your chocolate sauce. To do this place your chocolate and milk into a small sized saucepan. Cook over low to medium heat until your chocolate is fully melted.

7. Then use a small sized bowl and whisk together your cornstarch and remaining milk until smooth in consistency. Pour into your saucepan and stir thoroughly to combine.

8. Pour this mixture into a small sized bowl for serving and serve with your waffles. Coat your waffles with some sugar and cinnamon and enjoy.

Chocolate Chip and Pumpkin Waffles

These delicious waffles are packed full of pumpkin and chocolate chips, making it a dish that you are going to fall in love with. Topped off with some chocolate chips, pecans and maple syrup.

Makes: 6 Servings

Total Prep Time: 25 Minutes

Ingredients:

- 1 ½ Cups of Flour, Whole Wheat Variety and White in Color
- 1 tsp. of Baker's Style Baking Soda
- 1 ½ tsp. of Cinnamon, Ground
- 1/8 tsp. of Nutmeg
- 1 Cup of Pumpkin, Puree Variety
- ¼ Cup of Honey, Raw
- 1 Egg, Large in Size
- ½ Cup of Greek Yogurt, Plain and Nonfat
- 1/3 Cup of Milk, Vanilla and Almond Variety and Unsweetened
- ½ Cup of Chocolate Chips, Your Favorite Kind
- ¼ Cup of Pecans, Finely Chopped and Optional

Directions:

1. Use a medium sized bowl and whisk together your flour, baking soda, ground cinnamon and nutmeg until evenly mixed. Set this mixture aside for later use.

2. Then use a separate medium sized bowl and mix together your pumpkin, raw honey, eggs, milk and yogurt. Whisk until smooth in consistency.

3. Add your wet mixture into your dry mixture and stir thoroughly to combine.

4. Gently fold in your chocolate chips, making sure that you do not over stir your batter.

5. Once your batter is ready pour at least one fourth cup of your batter onto your waffle iron and cook for at least 5 minutes or until golden brown in color. Repeat until all of your batter has been used up.

6. Serve with your favorite maple syrup and enjoy.

French Toast Blueberry Cheesecake Waffles

This is a delicious breakfast dish that you can serve whenever you are having guests stay in your home. For the tastiest results I highly recommend serving this dish with some fresh jam and fresh fruits.

Makes: 4 Servings

Total Prep Time: 20 Minutes

Ingredients for Your Cheesecake Spread:

- 4 Ounces of Cream Cheese, Reduced in Fat
- 1/3 Cup of Sugar, Powdered Variety
- ½ tsp. of Vanilla, Pure

Ingredients for Your Filling:

- 1/3 Cup of Jam, Blueberry Variety
- ½ Cup of Blueberries, Fresh

Ingredients for Your French Toast Dip:

- 8 Slices of Raisin Bread, Cinnamon Variety
- 1 Egg, Large in Size
- 1/3 Cup of Milk, Whole
- ½ tsp. of Vanilla, Pure

Directions:

1. The first thing that you want to do is combine your cream cheese, powdered sugar and pure vanilla and in a small sized bowl until evenly mixed. Set this mixture aside for later use.

2. Then lay out your slices of bread and spread your cream cheese mixture on at least four of them.

3. On your remaining 4 slices top with your jam and blueberries. Then bring your tops of your sandwiches with your berry jam and blueberry mixture to your other slices of bread with your cream cheese mixture.

4. Then use a small sized bowl and combine your eggs, milk and pure vanilla for your dip.

5. Preheat a waffle iron to high heat. Once it is hot enough dip your sandwiches into your dip and place onto your waffle iron and cook for at least 5 minutes or until golden brown in color. Repeat until all of your sandwiches have been cooked.

6. Sprinkle with some powdered sugar and serve whenever you are ready.

Cinnamon Roll Style Waffles

Do you love the taste of cinnamon rolls? Do you love waffles? If you love both, then I know you are going to love this recipe. These waffles taste exactly like a cinnamon roll, making it the perfect breakfast treat to serve up for your pickiest eaters.

Makes: 4 to 6 Servings

Total Prep Time: 25 Minutes

Ingredients:

- 2 Cups of Flour, All Purpose Variety
- 1 tsp. of Salt, For Taste
- ½ tsp. of Baker's Style Baking Soda
- 3 tsp. of Cinnamon, Ground
- 2 Eggs, Large in Size and White and Yolks Separated
- 1/8 tsp. of Cream of Tartar
- 1 ¾ Cup of Buttermilk, Whole
- ¼ Cup of Butter, Fully Melted
- 2 Tbsp. of Maple Syrup, Your Favorite Kind
- 1 Tbsp. of Vanilla, Pure

Ingredients for Your Cream Cheese Glaze:

- 4 Tbsp. of Butter, Unsalted Variety
- 2 Ounces of Cream Cheese, Warm
- ¾ Cup of Sugar, Powdered Variety

- ½ tsp. of Vanilla, Pure

Directions:

1. Use a large sized bowl and stir together your flour, baking soda, dash of salt and ground cinnamon until evenly mixed. Set this mixture aside for later use

2. Then use a small sized bowl and beat together your egg whites with your cream of tartar using an electric mixer until peaks begin to form. Set this mixture aside.

3. Then using medium sized bowl beat together your egg yolks, whole buttermilk and melted butter. Add in your syrup and vanilla and set aside for later use.

4. Make a well in the center of your flour mixture and add in your egg yolk mixture. Mix until thoroughly combined. Gently fold in your egg whites.

5. Once your batter is ready pour at least one fourth cup of your batter onto your waffle iron and cook for at least 5 minutes or until golden brown in color. Repeat until all of your batter has been used up.

6. Make your cream cheese glaze. To do this beat together your butter, cream cheese, sugar and vanilla until evenly mixed. Pour over your waffles and enjoy whenever you are ready.

Lemon and Blueberry Crumb Cake Waffles

If you are looking for a delicious treat to serve up for Mother's Day, this is one recipe you need to try making. It is fancier than most waffle recipes out there and it will certainly impress your mother or wife on this special day.

Makes: 8 to 10 Servings

Total Prep Time: 13 Minutes

Ingredients:

- 1, 21 Ounce Cinnamon Swirl Crumb Cake and Muffin Mix, Dried
- ¼ Cup of Lemon Juice, Fresh
- ½ Cup of Water, Warm
- 1/3 Cup of Oil
- 1 Egg, Large in Size
- 1 Cup of Blueberries, Fresh
- 1 Lemon, Fresh and Zest Only

Directions:

1. The first thing that you want to do is preheat a waffle iron to high heat and spray with a generous amount of cooking spray.

2. Then use a large sized mixing bowl and add in all of your cake mix, half of your crumb topping that comes with the cake mix, fresh lemon juice, oil, water and egg. Stir thoroughly until evenly combined.

3. Once your batter is ready pour at least one fourth cup of your batter onto your waffle iron and cook for at least 5 minutes or until golden brown in color. Repeat until all of your batter has been used up.

4. Top off your cooked waffles with your crumb topping and serve with your favorite maple syrup.

Gingerbread and Yogurt Waffles

Regardless if you are looking for a special holiday treat or a sweet tasting dessert, this is the perfect dish for you to make. Serve with a warm and sweet tasting glaze, I know this is one dish you will want to make over and over again.

Makes: 5 Servings

Total Prep Time: 15 Minutes

Ingredients for Your Waffles:

- 1 Cup of Flour, All Purpose Variety
- ¾ Cup of Flour, Whole Wheat Variety
- ¼ Cup of Brown Sugar, Light and Packed
- 1 Tbsp. of Baker's Style Baking Powder
- 1 tsp. of Cinnamon, Ground
- 1 tsp. of Ginger, Ground
- ½ tsp. of Salt, For Taste
- ½ Cup of Butter, Fully Melted
- ¼ Cup of Molasses
- 1 Cup of Milk, Whole
- ½ Cup of Yogurt, Plain Variety
- 3 Eggs, Large in Size and Beaten

Ingredients for Your Sugar Glaze:

- 2 Cups of Sugar, Powdered Variety
- ½ tsp. of Vanilla, Pure
- ¼ Cup of Milk, Whole

Directions:

1. The first thing that you want to do is mix together all of your flours, light and packed brown sugar, baking powder, ginger, cinnamon and dash of salt in a large sized bowl until evenly mixed.

2. Make a well in the center of your mixture and add in your butter, molasses, whole milk, eggs and yogurt. Stir again until smooth in consistency.

3. Next heat up a waffle iron to high heat and spray with a generous amount of cooking spray.

4. Once your batter is ready pour at least one fourth cup of your batter onto your waffle iron and cook for at least 5 minutes or until golden brown in color. Repeat until all of your batter has been used up.

5. Then make your glaze. To do this use a small sized bowl and whisk together your sugar, vanilla and your milk. Pour your glaze over your cooked waffles. Serve right away and enjoy.

Nutella Packed Waffles

These tasty and fluffy waffles are stuffed full of Nutella filling, making them perfect for a delicious breakfast treat to enjoy every morning. Feel free to serve this waffle dish with a drizzling of Nutella to make it truly delicious.

Makes: 8 Servings

Total Prep Time: 10 Minutes

Ingredients:

- 1 Can of Pillsbury Biscuit Dough, Original Variety
- 8 Tbsp. of Nutella Spread, Your Favorite Kind

Directions:

1. The first thing that you want to do is preheat a waffle iron to high heat and spray with a generous amount of cooking spray.

2. Then cut one section of your biscuit dough and break in half. Flatten each piece of dough into a large sized circle.

3. Add a spoonful of your Nutella right into the center and top off with a second round of dough. Crimp the edges with a fork to seal

4. Place your dough discs onto your waffle iron and cook until golden brown in color. Repeat until all of your dough has been used up.

5. Drizzle some warm Nutella over the top and serve right away.

Decadent Tiramisu Waffles

Here is yet another dessert style and decadent style waffle recipe that you are going to love. For the tastiest results I highly recommend serving these treats with some fresh coffee.

Makes: 8 Servings

Total Prep Time: 45 Minutes

Ingredients for Your Waffles:

- 6 Eggs, Large in Size and Separated
- 1/8 tsp. of cream of Tartar
- ¾ Cup of Sugar, Granulated Variety and Evenly Divided
- 1 ½ Cups of Flour, All Purpose Variety
- ½ tsp. of Baker's Style Baking Powder
- 1 tsp. of Vanilla, Pure
- ¼ tsp. of Salt, For Taste

Ingredients for Your Filling:

- 1 Cup of Mascarpone Cheese
- ½ Cup of Sugar, Granulated Variety
- ¼ tsp. of Vanilla, Pure
- 2 Cups of Cream, Heavy Variety
- 1 Cup of Espresso, Brewed and Warm
- Some Cocoa Powder, For Dusting
- Some Chocolate Curls, For Garnish

Directions:

1. The first thing that you will want to do is mix all of your ingredients for your waffles together in a large sized bowl until evenly mixed.

2. Then preheat a waffle iron to high heat. Grease with a generous amount of cooking spray.

3. Once your batter is ready pour at least one fourth cup of your batter onto your waffle iron and cook for at least 5 minutes or until golden brown in color. Repeat until all of your batter has been used up.

4. Prepare your filling next. To do this use a large sized bowl and mix together all of your ingredients for your filling until evenly incorporated and thick in consistency.

5. Place half of your brewed espresso into a small sized pie pan. Dip each waffle into your espresso and stack on a serving plate, making sure to spread your filling in between each waffle.

6. Top with your remaining filling, powdered cocoa and chocolate shavings over the top. Serve right away and enjoy.

Classic Belgian Waffles

Here is a traditional and classic waffle recipe that you are going to love, especially if you are looking for a large and comforting breakfast for the entire family to enjoy. This is as classic as it gets when it comes to waffle recipes.

Makes: 4 Servings

Total Prep Time: 20 Minutes

Ingredients:

- 1 ½ Cups of Flour, All Purpose Variety
- ½ Cup of Cornstarch
- 1 tsp. of Baker's Style Baking Powder
- ½ tsp. of Baker's Style Baking Soda
- ½ tsp. of Salt, For Taste
- 1 ½ Cups of Buttermilk, Whole
- ½ Cup of Milk, Whole
- 6 Tbsp. of Oil, Vegetable Variety
- ½ tsp. of Vanilla, Pure
- 2 Eggs, Large in Size, Whites and Yolks Separated
- 3 Tbsp. of Sugar, White in Color

Directions:

1. The first thing that you will want to do is mix all of your ingredients together in a large sized bowl until evenly mixed.

2. Then preheat a waffle iron to high heat. Grease with a generous amount of cooking spray.

3. Once your batter is ready pour at least one fourth cup of your batter onto your waffle iron and cook for at least 5 minutes or until golden brown in color. Repeat until all of your batter has been used up.

4. Serve your waffles warm with your favorite maple syrup and some butter. Enjoy!

Tasty Cornmeal and Blackberry Waffles

This is a super decadent waffle treat that is incredibly soft and delicious to enjoy. Serve this waffle dish with some blackberry compote and savory whipped cream to make a treat that you will want to enjoy every morning.

Makes: 4 Servings

Total Prep Time: 30 Minutes

Ingredients:

- 1 Cup of Flour, All Purpose Variety
- 1 Cup of Cornmeal, Stone Ground Variety and Yellow in Color
- 2 tsp. of Baker's Style Baking Powder
- ½ tsp. of Baker's Style Baking Soda
- 14 tsp. of Salt, For Taste
- 2 Cups of Buttermilk, Whole
- 2 Eggs, Large in Size, Beaten Lightly
- ¼ Cup of Honey, Raw
- 1 tsp. of Vanilla, Pure
- 4 Tbsp. of Butter, Unsalted Variety and Fully Melted

Ingredients for Your Black Compote:

- 16 Ounces of Blackberries, Fresh

- 2 Tbsp. of Sugar, White in Color
- 1 Tbsp. of Water, Warm

Directions:

1. The first thing that you want to do is preheat your waffle iron. While your waffle iron is heating up grease it with a generous amount of cooking spray.

2. Then use a large sized bowl and whisk together your cornmeal, baking soda and powder, dash of salt and flour until evenly mixed.

3. Add in your buttermilk, honey, pure vanilla, and eggs. Stir thoroughly until evenly combined before adding in your butter.

4. Once your batter is ready pour at least one fourth cup of your batter onto your waffle iron and cook for at least 5 minutes or until golden brown in color. Repeat until all of your batter has been used up.

5. Next mix together your blackberries, sugar and water into a small sized saucepan. Place over medium heat and cook for 5 minutes or until your berries are soft to the touch. Remove from heat.

6. Top your waffles with your blackberry compote and a dash of whipped cream. Serve right away and enjoy.

Decadent Red Velvet Waffles

If you are a huge waffle lover and are looking for a creative and tasty dish to enjoy in the morning, then this is the perfect dish for you to make. This dish is the best dish to serve up for Halloween, Valentine's Day or Christmas morning.

Makes: 6 Servings

Total Prep Time: 25 Minutes

Ingredients:

- 2 Cups of Flour, All Purpose Variety
- 1 tsp. of Baker's Style Baking Soda
- 1 tsp. of Baker's Style Baking Powder
- ½ tsp. of Salt, For Taste
- 4 Tbsp. of Butter, Fully Melted
- ¼ Cup of Brown Sugar Light and Packed
- 3 Eggs, Large in Size and Separated
- 2 Cups of Buttermilk, Whole
- 1 ½ Tbsp. of Cocoa Powder, Unsweetened Variety
- 1 Tbsp. of Food Coloring, Red in Color

Directions:

1. First preheat your oven to 250 degrees as well as preheat a waffle iron to high heat.

2. While both are heating up mix together all of your ingredients in a large sized bowl until moist.

3. Grease your waffle iron with a generous amount of cooking spray.

4. Once your batter is ready pour at least one fourth cup of your batter onto your waffle iron and cook for at least 5 minutes or until golden brown in color. Repeat until all of your batter has been used up.

5. Serve with your favorite maple syrup and some butter and enjoy. Keep your extra waffles warm in your preheated oven.

Dark Chocolate Waffles

Are you a huge fan of chocolate and have been looking for the perfect way to satisfy your strong chocolate cravings? For the tastiest results I highly recommend drizzling your favorite kind of peanut butter over the top of these waffles to make it truly delicious.

Makes: 6 Servings

Total Prep Time: 40 Minutes

Ingredients:

- 2 Cups of Flour, All Purpose Variety
- ½ Cup of Cocoa Powder, Unsweetened Variety
- ¼ Cup of Brown Sugar, Light and Packed
- 2 tsp. of Baker's Style Baking Powder
- 1 tsp. of Baker's Style Baking Soda
- 1 tsp. of Salt, For Taste
- 3 Eggs, Large in Size and Separated
- 2 Cups of Buttermilk, Whole
- ½ Cup of Olive Oil, Extra Virgin Variety
- 1 tsp. of Vanilla, Pure
- 6 Ounces of Chocolate, Bittersweet Variety and Chopped Finely
- Some Cooking Spray
- Some Butter, For Serving
- Some Maple Syrup, For Serving

Directions:

1. First preheat your oven to 250 degrees as well as preheat a waffle iron to high heat.

2. While both are heating up mix together all of your ingredients in a large sized bowl until moist.

3. Grease your waffle iron with a generous amount of cooking spray.

4. Once your batter is ready pour at least one fourth cup of your batter onto your waffle iron and cook for at least 5 minutes or until golden brown in color. Repeat until all of your batter has been used up.

5. Serve with your favorite maple syrup, butter and drizzle of peanut butter. Keep your extra waffles warm in your preheated oven.

Pizza Stuffed Waffles

This is a waffle dish that I know you are going to want to make for lunch or for dinner. It makes for a delicious treat that you can serve up every day if you want to.

Makes: 4 Servings

Total Prep Time: 15 Minutes

Ingredients:

- 1, 16.3 Ounce Can of Pillsbury Biscuits
- 8 Slices of Mozzarella Cheese, Thinly Sliced
- 1/3 Cup of Pepperoni Slices, Mini Variety
- 2 Cups of Pizza Sauce, Organic Variety

Directions:

1. The first thing that you are going to want to do is cut each piece of your biscuits in half and roll into a large sized circle.

2. Top half of your circles with your pizza sauce, pepperoni slices and mozzarella cheese. Top with your remaining dough slices and crimp the edges with a fork.

3. Then preheat your waffle iron to high heat. Spray with a generous amount of cooking spray.

4. Once it is hot enough add in your biscuits one at a time and cook until golden in color. Remove and repeat with your remaining pizza rolls.

5. Serve with some pizza sauce as a dipping sauce and enjoy while piping hot.

Breakfast Time Chicken and Waffle Sandwiches

If you are looking for a more filling dish to enjoy in the morning, you can't go wrong with this recipe. This is the perfect dish for you to make especially if you are looking for a sandwich to bring along with you.

Makes: 1 Serving

Total Prep Time: 25 Minutes

Ingredients:

- 1 Chicken Breasts, Pounded
- 2 Cups of Buttermilk, Whole
- 2 Cups of Flour, All Purpose Variety
- 2 tsp. + ¼ tsp. of Salt, For Taste
- 1 tsp. of Cayenne Pepper
- Some Oil, Vegetable Variety
- 1 Tbsp. of Sugar, White
- 1 tsp. of Baker's Style Baking Powder
- ½ tsp. of Baker's Style Baking Soda
- 2 Eggs, Large in Size and Evenly Divided
- ¼ Cup + ½ Tbsp. of Butter, Fully Melted
- 1 Tbsp. of Honey, Raw
- 1 Tbsp. of Hot Sauce, Your Favorite Kind

Directions:

1. First place your chicken into 1 cup of your buttermilk and allow to marinate overnight.

2. The next morning mix together your flour with a dash of salt and cayenne pepper in a small sized bowl until evenly mixed.

3. Then dip your marinated chicken into your flour mixture until thoroughly coated on each side. Place back into your marinade and roll into your flour for a second time.

4. Next heat up some oil over high heat and once the oil is hot enough fry your chicken for at least 5 to 7 minutes or until fully cooked through. Remove and set aside to drain.

5. Then make your waffles. To do this preheat a waffle iron to high heat. While your waffle iron is heating up mix together flour, white sugar, baking powder and soda and dash of salt in a large sized bowl.

6. Add in your buttermilk and your remaining melted butter and stir until your mixture is moist.

7. Grease your waffle iron with a generous amount of cooking spray.

8. Once your batter is ready pour at least one fourth cup of your batter onto your waffle iron and cook for at least 5 minutes or until golden brown in color. Repeat until all of your batter has been used up.

9. Then melt some more butter in a large sized pan placed over medium heat. Once it is hot enough add in your egg and fry until your egg white is set.

10. Use a small sized bowl and mix together your hot sauce and honey until evenly mixed.

11. To assemble your sandwiches, place your chicken onto your waffle and drizzle your hot sauce over the top. Top off with your fried egg followed by another waffle and serve right away. Enjoy.

Decadent Fudge Waffles

This waffle recipe is the ultimate dessert breakfast dish that you can make. For the tastiest results I highly recommend serving this dish with some ice cream and fudge drizzled over the top to make the ultimate treat.

Makes: 10 Waffles

Total Prep Time: 40 Minutes

Ingredients:

- 2 Eggs, Large in Size and Warm
- 4 Tbsp. of Butter, Fully Melted and Cooled
- 1 tsp. of Vanilla, Pure
- 1 Cup of Buttermilk, Whole
- 1 Cup of Flour, All Purpose Variety
- ¾ Cup of Sugar, Granulated Variety
- ½ Cup of Cocoa Powder, Unsweetened Variety
- ½ tsp. of Baker's Style Baking Powder
- ½ tsp. of Baker's Style Baking Soda
- ¼ tsp. of Salt, For Taste
- ¼ tsp. of Nutmeg
- ½ Cup of Chocolate Chips, Miniature Variety

Directions:

1. First preheat your oven to 250 degrees as well as preheat a waffle iron to high heat.

2. While both are heating up mix together all of your ingredients in a large sized bowl until moist. Remember to gently fold in your chocolate chips to prevent over mixing.

3. Grease your waffle iron with a generous amount of cooking spray.

4. Once your batter is ready pour at least one fourth cup of your batter onto your waffle iron and cook for at least 5 minutes or until golden brown in color. Repeat until all of your batter has been used up.

5. Serve with your favorite maple syrup and some butter and enjoy. Keep your extra waffles warm in your preheated oven.

Delicious Maple Bacon Waffles

Here is yet another waffle recipe that I know you are going to fall in love with. It is great for those who are looking for a filling and wholesome meal to enjoy on a lazy Sunday evening.

Makes: 4 Servings

Total Prep Time: 14 Minutes

Ingredients:

- 1 ¼ Cup of Flour, All Purpose Variety
- 1 Tbsp. of Baker's Style Baking Powder
- 1 Tbsp. of Sugar, White
- ½ tsp. of Salt, For Taste
- 3 Eggs, Large in Size and Lightly Beaten
- 6 Tbsp. of Butter, Fully Melted
- 1 ½ Cup of Milk, Whole
- 2 tsp. of Maple Extract, Pure
- Candied Bacon, Finely Chopped
- Maple Flavored Whipped Cream

Directions:

1. First preheat your oven to 250 degrees as well as preheat a waffle iron to high heat.

2. While both are heating up mix together all of your ingredients in a large sized bowl until moist.

3. Grease your waffle iron with a generous amount of cooking spray.

4. Once your batter is ready pour at least one fourth cup of your batter onto your waffle iron and cook for at least 5 minutes or until golden brown in color. Repeat until all of your batter has been used up.

5. Serve with your favorite maple syrup and some more bacon. Keep your extra waffles warm in your preheated oven.

Banana Bread Style Waffles

With this dish you can start off your morning the perfect way. Top this dish with some warm maple syrup and a dollop of whipped cream, making this the ultimate breakfast dish to serve up.

Makes: 5 Servings

Total Prep Time: 20 Minutes

Ingredients:

- 2 Cups of Flour, All Purpose Variety
- 2 Tbsp. of Sugar, White in Color
- 1 tsp. of Baker's Style Baking Powder
- ½ tsp. of Baker's Style Baking Soda
- ½ tsp. of Salt, For Taste
- ¼ tsp. of Cinnamon, Ground
- Dash of Nutmeg
- 1 Cup of Milk, Whole
- 2 Bananas, Ripe and Mashed
- 2 Eggs, Large in Size and Beaten Lightly
- ¼ Cup of Oil, Vegetable Variety
- 1 tsp. of Vanilla, Pure
- ¼ Cup of Walnuts, Finely Chopped

Directions:

1. First preheat your oven to 250 degrees as well as preheat a waffle iron to high heat.

2. While both are heating up mix together all of your ingredients in a large sized bowl until moist.

3. Grease your waffle iron with a generous amount of cooking spray.

4. Once your batter is ready pour at least one fourth cup of your batter onto your waffle iron and cook for at least 5 minutes or until golden brown in color. Repeat until all of your batter has been used up.

5. Serve with your favorite maple syrup, whipped cream, fresh banana slices and enjoy. Keep your extra waffles warm in your preheated oven.

Blueberry Style Muffin Waffles

If you love the taste of blueberry muffins and waffles, this is going to be one dish you need to make for yourself. It is incredibly easy to make and great for those who live on a budget.

Makes: 6 Servings

Total Prep Time: 30 Minutes

Ingredients:

- ½ Cup of Oil, Vegetable Variety
- 1 Cup of Milk, Whole
- 2 Eggs, Large in Size and Beaten Lightly
- 1 Cup of Sugar, White
- 1 ¾ Cups of Flour, All Purpose Variety
- 1 tsp. of Baker's Style Baking Powder
- 1 Cup of Blueberries, Fresh

Directions:

1. First preheat your oven to 250 degrees as well as preheat a waffle iron to high heat.

2. While both are heating up mix together all of your ingredients in a large sized bowl until moist. Remember to gently fold in your blueberries to prevent mashing them in the process.

3. Grease your waffle iron with a generous amount of cooking spray.

4. Once your batter is ready pour at least one fourth cup of your batter onto your waffle iron and cook for at least 5 minutes or until golden brown in color. Repeat until all of your batter has been used up.

5. Serve with your favorite maple syrup and some butter and enjoy. Keep your extra waffles warm in your preheated oven.

Conclusion

Well, there you have it!

Hopefully by the end of this book you have discovered the wonder that are waffles and have learned more about them in the process. Inside of this book I hope you were able to learn a few helpful tips to making the most delicious waffles possible as well as found the over 25 different recipes I have given you to be some of the most delicious you have ever come across.

So, what is the next step for you?

The next step for you to take is to begin making all of these recipes you have found in this book. Once you have done that and have impressed your friends and family, it is time for you to begin making your own waffle recipes from scratch. Don't worry, I have complete faith in you.

Good luck!

Author's Afterthoughts

Thanks ever so much to each of my cherished readers for investing the time to read this book!

I know you could have picked from many other books but you chose this one. So a big thanks for downloading this book and reading all the way to the end.

If you enjoyed this book or received value from it, I'd like to ask you for a favor. Please take a few minutes to post an honest and heartfelt review on Amazon.com. Your support does make a difference and helps to benefit other people.

Thanks for your Reviews!

Rachael Rayner

CPSIA information can be obtained
at www.ICGtesting.com
Printed in the USA
BVHW032015040719
552615BV00001B/152/P